BOOK 4

Grand SOLO FOR Christmas

8 Arrangements for Early Intermediate Pianists

Melody Bober

When I was a young piano student, I always looked forward to the Christmas season. I knew that I would receive new Christmas solos from my teacher. Each year the pieces were a little harder, and that was sometimes challenging, but they were always exciting to practice and perform. Christmas is a fun time of year filled with events that create a lifetime of memories. I remember the huge Christmas tree at my grandparents' house, homemade holiday treats, the reading of the Christmas story from the Bible, and, of course, Santa's visit! The Christmas music was always the highlight for me and truly captured the spirit of the season.

In that spirit, I have written *Grand Solos for Christmas*, Book 4, to provide a memorable Christmas experience for today's students at the piano. Students can learn familiar Christmas music that will help them progress technically and musically. I have included some of my holiday favorites in the hope that they will become favorites of those who perform them as well.

I sincerely hope that you will enjoy these *Grand Solos for Christmas.* Merry Christmas!

CONTENTS

Alfred Music
P.O. Box 10003
Van Nuys, CA 91410-0003
alfred.com

ISBN-10: 1-4706-2956-9
ISBN-13: 978-1-4706-2956-4

Cover Photo
Christmas background: © Shutterstock.com / k r e f

Jingle Bells

James Pierpont
Arr. Melody Bober

Angels from the Realms of Glory

Henry T. Smart
Arr. Melody Bober

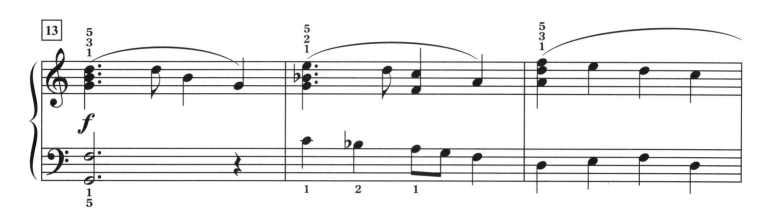

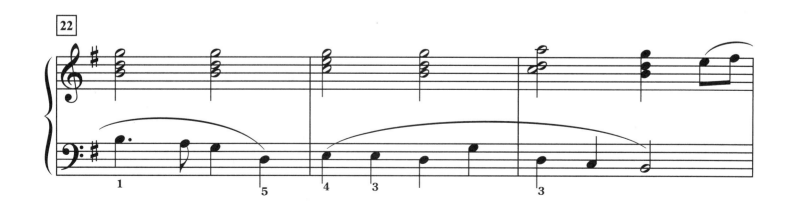

Pat-a-pan

Bernard de la Monnoye
Arr. Melody Bober

While Shepherds Watched Their Flocks

George Frideric Handel
Arr. Melody Bober

Silent Night

Franz Grüber
Arr. Melody Bober

Joy to the World

Lowell Mason
Arr. Melody Bober

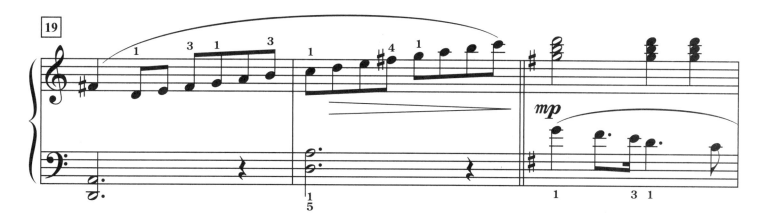

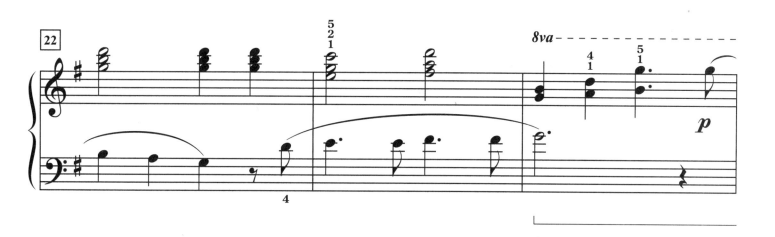

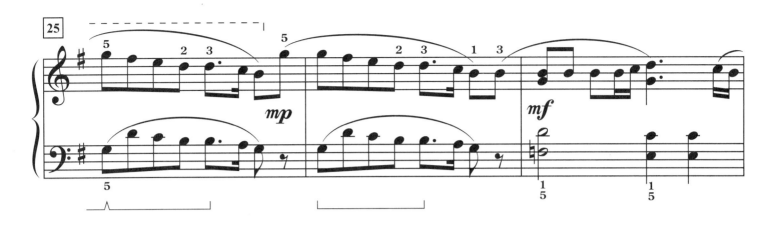

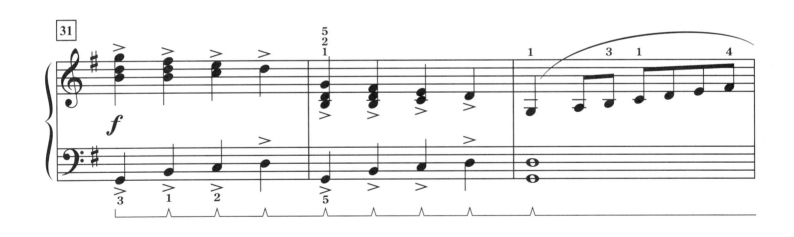

The First Noel

Traditional English Carol
Arr. Melody Bober

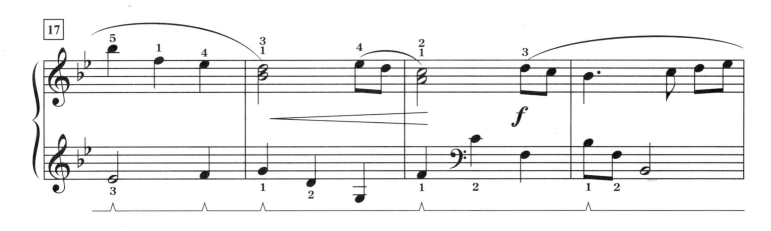

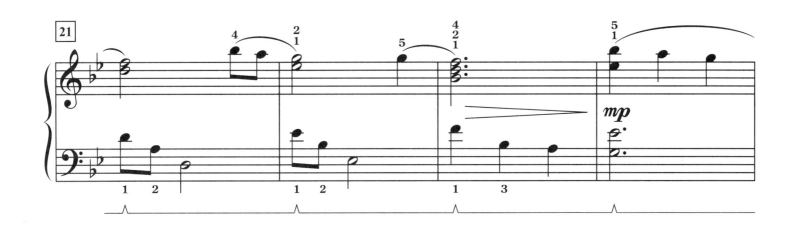

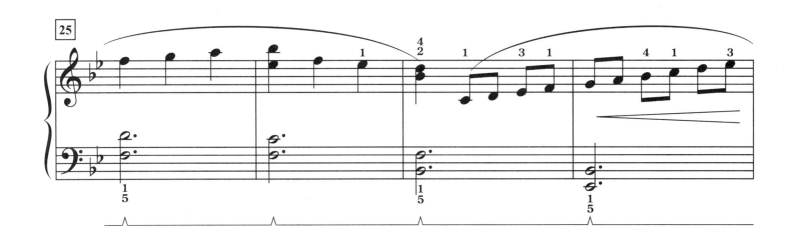

Slower (♩ = 80)

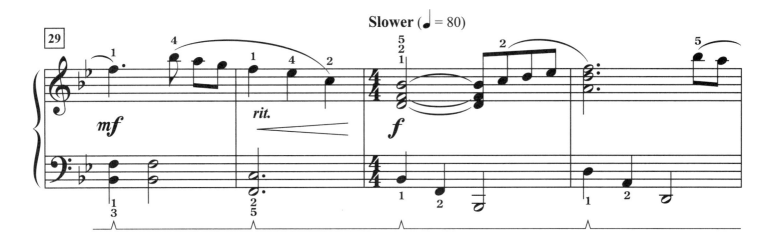

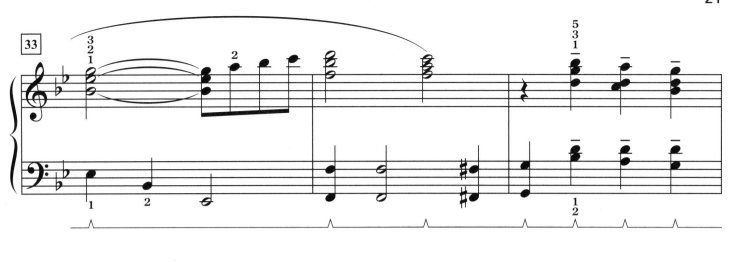

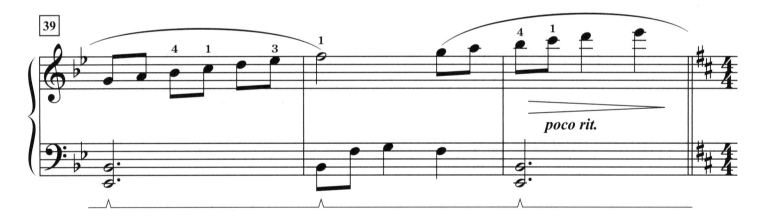

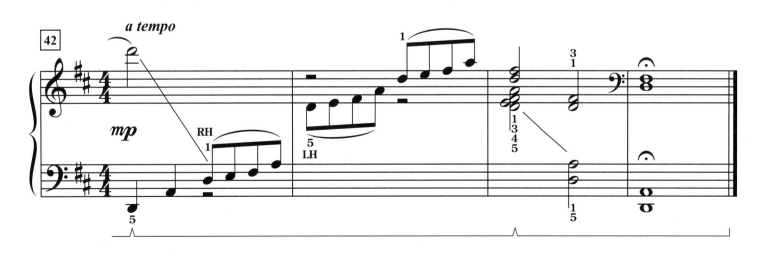

O Come, All Ye Faithful

John Francis Wade
Arr. Melody Bober

Spirited (♩ = 96)

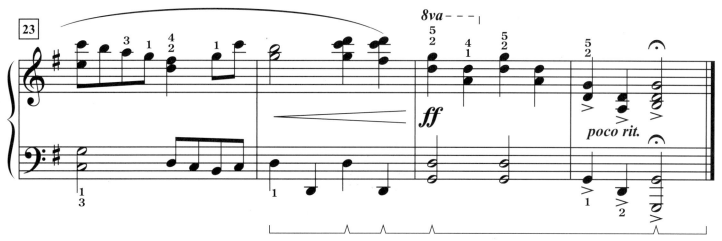